Elkin, Judith
 Japanese family.—(Beans)
 1. Tokyo (Japan)—Social life and customs—
Juvenile literature
 I. Title
 952′.135048   DS896.5
 ISBN 0–7136–2816–2

A & C Black (Publishers) Limited
35 Bedford Row, London WC1R 4JH

© 1986 A & C Black (Publishers) Limited

Acknowledgements
The map is by Tony Garrett
The Author and publisher would like to thank the
Tomita family and Yoko Toyokazi for their help and
advice.

Filmset by August Filmsetting, Haydock, St. Helens.
Printed in Hong Kong by Dai Nippon Printing Co. Ltd.

Japanese Family

Judith Elkin

Photographs by Stuart Atkin

A & C Black · London

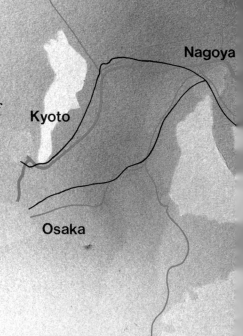

Nagoya

Kyoto

Osaka

Hallo! My name is Daisuke Tomita. I'm twelve years old and I live with my parents and brother. We've just been shopping in Tokyo so we're all dressed up. Well, I wear my favourite T-shirt most of the time, but all the others are in their best clothes.

Tokyo is usually very crowded, although it's quite empty today. That's because it's Sunday so some of the streets are closed to traffic. Most people in Tokyo live in small apartments with very little space and no garden. We used to live in a small apartment in the suburbs of Tokyo, but two years ago we moved to Higashi Matsuyama, about fifty kilometres from Tokyo. It's an industrial town but there are parks and lots of open spaces. When it's not cloudy we can even see Mount Fuji.

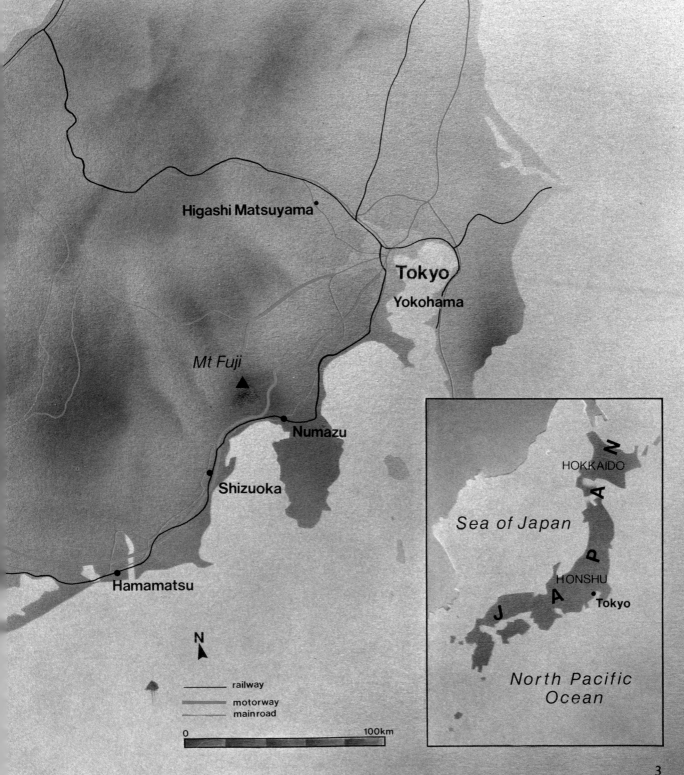

Higashi Matsuyama

Tokyo

Yokohama

Mt Fuji

Numazu

Shizuoka

Hamamatsu

N

railway
motorway
mainroad

0   100km

HOKKAIDO

Sea of Japan

HONSHU

Tokyo

*North Pacific
Ocean*

JAPAN

3

I'm in the sixth grade at school. I like kendo, swimming and baseball. I read a lot, especially about cars and trains. This is my brother Kengo who is seven and has just started at school. He likes reading comics. He's a great joker and is always dreaming up tricks to make everyone laugh. It drives me crazy.

Mum and Dad get up early every morning. In summer they get up at 5.30 to go jogging. In winter they get up later and Mum drives Dad to work. Kengo and I stay in bed as long as possible.

Dad works as a kacho, or section chief, in the offices of a large company called Diesel Kiki. The plant where Dad works produces hydraulic equipment, electronic devices and robots. The motto of the company is, 'Working to meet the needs of tomorrow under the slogan of HONESTY, ENTHUSIASM AND INGENUITY'. Dad drives us mad quoting it.

Kengo and I start walking to school at 7.50. We both go to Nishi Shogakko West Elementary School. It takes us about forty minutes to get there. We wear yellow hats for safety, they're part of our uniform. The labels on our jackets tell you our address, school year and class.

There are forty four children in my class. Our teacher's name is Mr Uchida but we call him 'sensei' which means teacher. He takes us for everything except art, calligraphy and music. My favourite subject is social studies and I hate maths. Kengo is the opposite, he likes maths and hates social studies.

One of the hardest things we have to study is the Japanese language. To be able to read and write it properly, we have to learn two thousand characters (called kanji), and two 48-letter alphabets called hiragana and katakana. You can see why it's difficult. Each kanji has to be written in a very particular way: in the right order and in the right direction using a thin brush and ink.

This is my name written in kanji and hiragana:

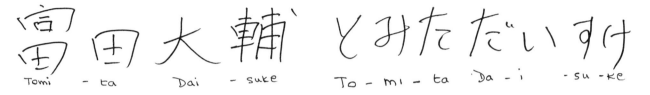

I'm not sure what the calligraphy sensei would make of it! Here is our calligraphy corrected by the sensei. Mine is the second from the left. The red rings are round the good bits, but he didn't like some of my brush strokes. He's even corrected my signature down the left hand side.

6

Dad won't be very pleased about some of my work when he comes to visit the school. He's a member of the Parent Teacher's Association, so he doesn't miss much, unfortunately. Everybody's parents have to visit school five times a year, and the sensei visits everyone at home once a year.

I'm glad when the calligraphy lesson is over, especially when we've got swimming next. In the summer we have swimming lessons twice a week in the school pool. I can do backstroke, breaststroke and crawl but I'm not so good at diving yet.

Swimming is the most popular lesson and we play about a lot afterwards. Michiko's towel says 'Friends always make life merrier – let's chat.' That suits her – she's always chattering.

We're always hungry after swimming. Lunch is
12.20 till 12.50. We eat in our classrooms and have
to wear white hats and aprons for cleanliness. The
food is brought in from outside the school but we
have to serve it out ourselves. We sit at the same
table for lunch for a whole term and our sensei
always eats with us.

The class leader for today, Kenji, sits at the sensei's
desk looking very important and unusually serious.
He has to say 'itadakimasu', which means 'good
eating', before we can start.

Today we've each got a carton of milk, fried noodles, bread, cheese and a tomato. We have my favourite curry rice once a month.

We're supposed to be very well behaved, especially at lunchtime, but sometimes I can't help teasing my best friend Takashi.

After lunch we clean our teeth and go to the toilet. The toilets are Japanese style, with a hole in the floor. We have a break for twenty five minutes, and after that we help to sweep up the classroom and corridor to get rid of all the crumbs and mess from lunch. Here's Kengo going off to clean his teeth. He goes everywhere with his girlfriend Yoko. She's forgotten to take off her lunch apron and hat.

Twice a week I go to the Dojo, which is the Martial Arts Centre, for Kendo training. Kendo is the oldest of the Japanese martial arts. It's based on the teachings and methods of sword fighting used by the samurai warriors hundreds of years ago. Kendo is now a very popular sport, and there are always films and serials about the samurai on TV.

When we've got changed, which is easier than it looks, we kneel and meditate for a few minutes to prepare our minds and bodies.

The training is very hard and very strict. You have to have the right attitude of mind – not easy! Footwork is vital. We use short, fast gliding steps and sometimes a jump to counter-attack. First we exercise without our helmets and then fully equipped.

Here we are, waiting for pairs practice. I am, as usual, the tall one at the back.

In contest practice we fight with bamboo swords like the samurai used in their exercises. You win the contest by striking the opponent's mask, arm or body, with just the right amount of force. Your body and sword have to be in the proper position, too. It's really hard to get them right all at the same time.

I enjoy kendo, and it's useful being so tall, but it is tiring. The Dojo has no heating or air conditioning so it's very hot in summer and freezing in winter. That's supposed to be good for our training.

We celebrate lots of festivals during the year. Each one has special traditions, decorations and food. Some are to do with the main religion in Japan which is Shinto, and others are Buddhist. Most people celebrate the festivals and ceremonies of both religions. Sometimes you can see people wearing traditional Japanese dress at the festivals. You don't often see anyone wearing a kimono except on special occasions.

The festival Kengo and I like best is the Boys' Festival. It's held on the fifth day of the fifth month, and it's a national holiday. On Boys' Day we usually visit the big Shinto shrine near Dad's factory.

There are hundreds of stalls and sideshows selling all kinds of things – masks, lanterns, toys, balloons, icecream, takeaway food and drink, almost everything you can think of. The man selling masks has got a cold so he's wearing a different sort of mask. Kengo says that he should have painted a funny face on it, to match the stall.

We have to purify our mouths and hands with water before we go into the shrine to pray. I pray for good marks at school and for getting better at calligraphy.

We've hung two huge carp outside our house
especially for Boys' Day. They are nearly as big as
the house and made of cloth. When the wind blows
they swell up and look as if they're swimming. The
carp stands for strength, energy and long life. We
hang them up to remind my brother and me that
boys should face up to difficulties with the same
spirit as the carp.

In Japan you have to take your shoes off as you go inside, and change into slippers called surippa. Kengo and I don't always bother to put on the surippa but Mum keeps reminding us to leave them by the door for guests.

In the guest room we have to go barefoot because the floor is covered with a special rush mat called tatami. We always go barefoot on tatami – that's the Japanese custom.

Also in the guest room is a display case where we put special things at festival times. At the moment we've put in a samurai helmet and a samurai doll and horse for Boys' Day.

We're watching TV in the sitting room by a low table called kotatsu. The table can be electrically heated in winter to keep your legs and feet warm. Kengo and I spend hours under it, eating and watching TV, and Kengo often falls asleep there. I love watching baseball on TV – you can usually see it on two or three channels every night.

The sitting room opens onto the kitchen. We eat breakfast there, but we have our other meals in the sitting room. Most of my friends watch breakfast TV and there's a good choice of serials to watch early in the morning, but Dad doesn't approve.

The kitchen's quite crowded. Mum cooks on gas rings in the corner. We don't have an oven because most of our food is fried, steamed or eaten raw. There are so many cafes that we eat out a lot, too.

When we eat at home we often have sushi, which is
rice and raw fish or vegetables. We usually order it
from a take-away, and it's delivered to the house.

My favourite meal is when we cook at table on a
hot-plate. All Mum has to do is give us the raw
ingredients – things like onions, pork, green peppers
and liver – and let us get on with it. We dip
everything into a special sauce before we eat it, and
finish off with noodles cooked on the hotplate.

I like any food, Japanese or Western. My favourites
are Japanese style curry rice, fried chicken,
Japanese cakes, hamburgers and anko, a kind of
sweet bean jam. Kengo eats anything except green
peppers which he really hates!

The door on the left of our kitchen leads to the bathroom and a small room where we get undressed. We always have two baths. First we wash outside the bath then swill all the soap off. We can splash water as much as we like because the bathroom's specially built for this and has a drain in the floor.

We get into the bath just to relax in the lovely clean water and, of course, everyone in the family can use it after us. Soon there won't be room for Kengo and me both together.

You might be wondering why we have leaves in the bath. They are iris leaves to purify us and give us strength. We don't usually play with leaves in the bath, but it's fun on Boys' Day.

The toilet is separate from the bathroom. We wear special toilet surippa there. So if I go from the tatami sitting room, through the kitchen to the toilet, I put my surippa on outside the sitting room to walk across the kitchen, and change into the toilet surippa outside the toilet. Then I do exactly the same going back. It sounds complicated but mostly you do it automatically.

Kengo and I share a bedroom which is just big enough for our bunk beds, bookshelves and desks. Kengo sleeps on the top. He never uses the ladder – the chest of drawers makes a better assault course. I usually do my homework after Kengo is asleep because it's too difficult to concentrate when he's playing about. I often have to do two or three hours homework a night.

We sometimes visit the local Buddhist temple, down
the road from our house. It's called the Yoshimi
Kannon temple, Kannon is the Buddhist goddess of
mercy.

It's always very peaceful inside – at least until we
get there. We waft smoke over our heads, to purify
us and give us good health. Then Kengo and I race
to the huge bronze statue of Kannon.

We like to get our fortunes from the omikuji machine. We have to pay about thirty yen, which is only a little bit of my pocket money. I am trying to read my fortune, but it's written in an old-fashioned classical style so I don't really understand it.

Kengo is trying to cheat by reading his fortune inside the machine and saving thirty yen. But the omikuji fortunes are written on pieces of paper tied round bamboo sticks, so he'll never manage it. When you've read your fortune, you tie the piece of paper to the branch of a tree in the temple grounds.

Kengo always stops to look at the statues of the mizukojizo. Jizo is the protector of small children and babies, so mothers hang bibs and baby clothes on the statues to pray for sick children to get better. It makes Kengo feel sad and quiet.

Many Japanese homes have Buddhist altars where you pray for dead relatives. Each time we visit Grandma in Kyoto, she opens up the altar which she has in a special display alcove. We bring offerings like fruit or small cakes to remember Grandad who died last year. That's his photograph on the altar. He was a very good artist and he printed his pictures with wood blocks. One of them is on the wall by the altar.

I like visiting Grandma because she's a good cook. She cooks very different food from Mum, because she took French cookery lessons. She likes to drink wine with her food, and I usually have a drop too.

Grandma makes very delicate paper dolls in the traditional Japanese style, and teaches other people how to do it. I love looking at the different designs of the handmade paper she collects for her dolls. She won't let Kengo go near her paper, in case he spoils any of it.

I like watching her make the dolls. It's very difficult because she has to make everything to exactly the right scale. The style and pattern of the kimonos is accurate, too. It is very delicate work and Grandma now has to wear strong glasses to see clearly.

The whole house is full of dolls. Grandad collected traditional dolls from all over Japan, and there are lots of dolls that Grandma has made.

My uncle lives in the old part of Tokyo, where Dad
was born. He still runs the family barber's shop
and we often go and visit him.

We like going into the city centre to have lunch.
Some of the cafes and bars put out tables and
chairs on the main streets on Sundays. We sit and
eat hamburgers and chips and watch the people go
by. Kengo and I are playing Jan-Ken-Pon!
(Scissors-Paper-Stone) to see who's going to pay
for a second glass of coke.

Kengo and I always want to go to Sunshine City which is a huge building with lots of different shops inside. It's sixty floors high and from the top you can see for miles. There are some binoculars, but you have to pay to use them. Dad says it's too expensive to do it very often.

We walk back to the station through Ueno Park. Sometimes we go to the zoo there. We love the Giant Pandas but so does everyone else and it looks too crowded to bother today. There are too many groups and parties. Instead we walk under the Torii gateway which leads to the shrine next to the park. Even that's crowded.

The shops stay open late at night and it would be good to wander round them when they're lit up. But we can't stay late – it's school tomorrow and I've still got some homework to do.